Victorious Bible Curriculum

THE BEGINNING (PART 1 OF 9)

God created a home for mankind, and placed us in it to tend and guard it as His image. When we rebelled, God promised a seed of the woman to one day restore creation — and preserved that seed when our violence filled the world.

THE PATRIARCHS (PART 2 OF 9)

God chose Abraham to be the custodian of the line through which the promised redeemer would come. Abraham's grandson Jacob became the father of the twelve tribes of Israel, a nation that would bless the whole earth.

THE EXODUS (PART 3 OF 9)

For 400 years, God grew Jacob's tiny family into a nation. Through Moses, He released them from slavery to give them a new home. Despite the faithless first generation's rebellion, their children would inherit the promised land.

CONQUEST AND JUDGMENT (PART 4 OF 9)

Under Joshua, the children of the exodus conquered the promised land. After they settled in, they fell into idolatry and suffered under foreign domination. Time after time, they needed God's deliverance through a head-crushing judge.

THE KINGDOM OF ISRAEL (PART 5 OF 9)

God used Israel's first kings, the vacillating Saul and the head-crusher David, to give Israel peace. Solomon built a prosperous kingdom, which then split and fell into idolatry. After 70 years' exile in Babylon, God restored them to the land.

THE COMING OF THE MESSIAH (PART 6 OF 9)

The long wait for the serpent-crushing redeemer came to an end with the birth of Jesus of Nazareth. Raised in Galilee and baptized in the Jordan, He began to proclaim the kingdom of God and demonstrate God's love and power.

THE MINISTRY OF JESUS (PART 7 OF 9)

The blind could see, the sick were healed, the dead raised. The kingdom of God was truly at hand. But the leaders of Israel rejected the One God had sent to save them from their sins and deliver them into God's kingdom.

JESUS' FINAL DAYS (PART 8 OF 9)

On Thursday, before His arrest, Jesus ate one final meal with His disciples. Then He was arrested, beaten, falsely accused, tried, convicted and crucified. But death could not hold Him and the grave could not contain Him.

THE BEGINNING OF THE CHURCH (PART 9 OF 9)

After His resurrection, Jesus' followers received the power of the Holy Spirit to disciple the nations of the world, baptizing them and teaching them all that Jesus had said. Christ's body grew and began to crush the enemy's head under her feet.

Copyright © 2017 by Joe Anderson and Tim Nichols

All rights reserved
Printed in the United States of America
First Edition

No part of this book may be reproduced in any form or by any electronic or mechanical means, including information storage and retrieval systems, except for brief quotations in printed reviews, without the prior permission of the author.

Unless otherwise indicated, all Scripture quotations are taken from the New King James Version®. Copyright © 1982 by Thomas Nelson, Inc. Used by permission. All rights reserved.

Scripture quotations marked (NIV) are taken from the Holy Bible, New International Version®, NIV®. Copyright © 1973, 1978, 1984, 2011 by Biblica, Inc.™ Used by permission of Zondervan. All rights reserved worldwide. www.zondervan.com The "NIV" and "New International Version" are trademarks registered in the United States Patent and Trademark Office by Biblica, Inc.™

Author's translation or paraphrase indicated by an asterisk after the reference.

Illustrations by Gustave Doré
Colorized and modified by William Britton

Praise for Headwaters Bible Curriculum

These lessons are not just a way to teach the Bible to middle school kids. As I read the lessons, I found both my head and my heart irresistibly engaged. Joe and Tim have opened the grace and truth of God's Word in a way that seriously lifts us towards Christ while nudging us outward towards the world. I recommend these studies for both devotional and motivational reading!

Dave Cheadle, President of the Rocky Mountain Classis, Reformed Church of America

While I have spent quite a bit of time studying the Bible myself, I find your ideas and themes to be real food for thought and they help tie together much of the story God is telling throughout... I've already talked with people about your curriculum and have recommended they look into it for their own families. I can't loan out my copy for their perusal, because I'm using it everyday!

Linda Kidder, Home Educator, Colorado

I LOVE THIS BOOK!!!! We're just finishing up the Garden narrative. We've had such fruitful discussions—I have been pleased with it in every way. In fact, I'm hoping our church will start using it. I haven't had any problems or difficulties using the curriculum, I ONLY have good things to say about it. In fact, I'm in danger of writing in all caps I'm so enthusiastic about it.

Leah Robinson, Home Educator, Texas

I am really enjoying having this resource to work from and steer our lessons!

Christy Johnson, Bible Teacher, Bingham Academy, Ethiopia

Our family actually loves the curriculum. My children are in 5th and 8th grade and the content has suited both of their levels perfectly. To this point we hadn't found a curriculum that taught the Bible at such a detailed level that has also kept the kids engaged. We've had to slow down on the materials because otherwise they would be through them well before the school year is up. We are planning on buying the rest of the series.

Chris Turner, Home Educator, Colorado

How to Use This Book

This series of little manuals walks you through the biblical Story from end to end. Just read. Here are a few things you might want to keep in mind as you read through the Story.

- Try to love the characters. God does....
- The story is written in such a way as to make sin look stupid, but remember that the characters are all real people. No matter how stupid the choice, a real person actually looked at the options and then picked that particular one for reasons that seemed pretty good at the time. Nobody gets up in the morning and says, "I'm going to make stupid life choices that people will be mocking for centuries." Try to see it from their point of view. Ask yourself, "Why did this look like a good idea at the time?" That's how you learn to recognize temptations. It's easy to see sinful and stupid choices for what they are in hindsight, but in the moment it's often very hard. So learn to think through what these choices looked like from the inside, in the heat of the moment — you'll be amazed what you learn about yourself.
- Pay attention to the patterns. We'll point out a bunch of them as we go through the Story, but try to spot them yourself, too. If you can learn to read the Word and see the patterns in the Story, you will become able to read the world around you and see the patterns in the story God is telling right now.
- In the Old Testament curriculum, every lesson came with a Psalm. Not all of the New Testament lessons do, but you should know enough about how to connect the Psalms to the Story that you can discover your own connections. If there is no Psalm provided, feel free to take some time to read through a few Psalms and try to find one that fits. You'll be surprised what you can learn.
- As with any book that talks about Scripture, don't necessarily take our word for anything. Imagine you're sitting in a living room or around a campfire with us, and we're just talking about the Story. You're free to disagree, correct, challenge our understanding. The Word is the authority, not us — so grab your Bible and look things up yourself.

You'll find a section labeled "Activities" following the lesson. The point of this section is to immerse you as deeply in the Story as possible, through prayer, meditation on the Story, and other exercises. The "Evaluation" questions at the end of each lesson will help you to check your understanding of the material.

For Small Group Leaders
Have everyone in the group read the lesson ahead of time. Depending on how involved your group is, you can have them engage some or all of the activities, or you can save those for group time when you're together. The evaluation questions might serve as discussion starters if the conversation lags.

Table of Contents

Unit 5 Jesus' Final Days 7
    Lesson 5.1 The Sending of the Seventy and the Fall of Satan 9
    Lesson 5.2 Jesus Raised Lazarus from the Dead 15
    Lesson 5.3 Jesus' Arrival in Jerusalem 23
    Lesson 5.4 Jesus Instituted Communion 31
    Lesson 5.5 Jesus Betrayed, Arrested and Forsaken 39
    Lesson 5.6 Jesus Tried and Convicted 45
    Lesson 5.7 Jesus' Crucifixion and Burial 53
    Lesson 5.8 Jesus' Resurrection and Ascension 61

UNIT 5: JESUS' FINAL DAYS

Jesus had been rejected by the very people He came to offer the kingdom to, but hope was not lost; a new people had been born who would carry on His mission after Jesus' ascension. Jesus knew what was to come and set His face resolutely toward Jerusalem; He was going there to die. But on His way, He made one more pass through the land of Israel and even ventured into Gentile territories. He sent out seventy of His disciples to announce His coming and give the people a final chance to repent. To the disciples' surprise, they had great success!

The disciples didn't understand that their success in the land was a foretaste of what was to come after Jesus was gone. So when Jesus headed to Judea after He heard that His friend Lazarus was dead, the disciples were greatly concerned that Jesus would get Himself killed. And rightfully so, for after Jesus raised Lazarus from the dead, the miracle was reported to the religious leaders in Jerusalem who plotted all the more to kill Him.

Jesus knew His fate, but nevertheless entered Jerusalem triumphantly on a donkey, as a king who had been victorious on the battlefield and was returning to sit on His throne. He spent His last free hours in fellowship with His disciples at the Passover meal, a meal with a rich history of communion with God. Jesus transformed that meal from a memorial of the exodus to a memorial of God's deliverance through Jesus Christ. Following the meal, He went to the garden of Gethsemane to prepare for His arrest. When Judas came and betrayed Him, Jesus willingly went before the religious leaders to be accused so that He might obey God to the point of death.

The religious leaders wanted Jesus dead more than anyone, but they didn't want to assume responsibility for His death, so they took Jesus before Pilate. Pilate didn't want to take responsibility either, but after trying to pass the buck, he finally complied with the wishes of the people and sent Jesus off to be crucified. Pilate washed his hands of the thing, while the people took responsibility for Jesus' blood.

The entirety of the Old Testament points toward the coming Messiah as the final head-crusher. Jesus' disciples were expecting Him to defeat their enemies and take His rightful place as King. Instead, Jesus was mocked, beaten, crucified and buried. He received the fate of the serpent in order to defeat the serpent once and for all. But the Story doesn't end there. When Jesus' body was put in the grave, His disciples thought that the end of their hope had come, but it was only the beginning. Jesus rose from the dead and appeared to many; therefore, we have hope.

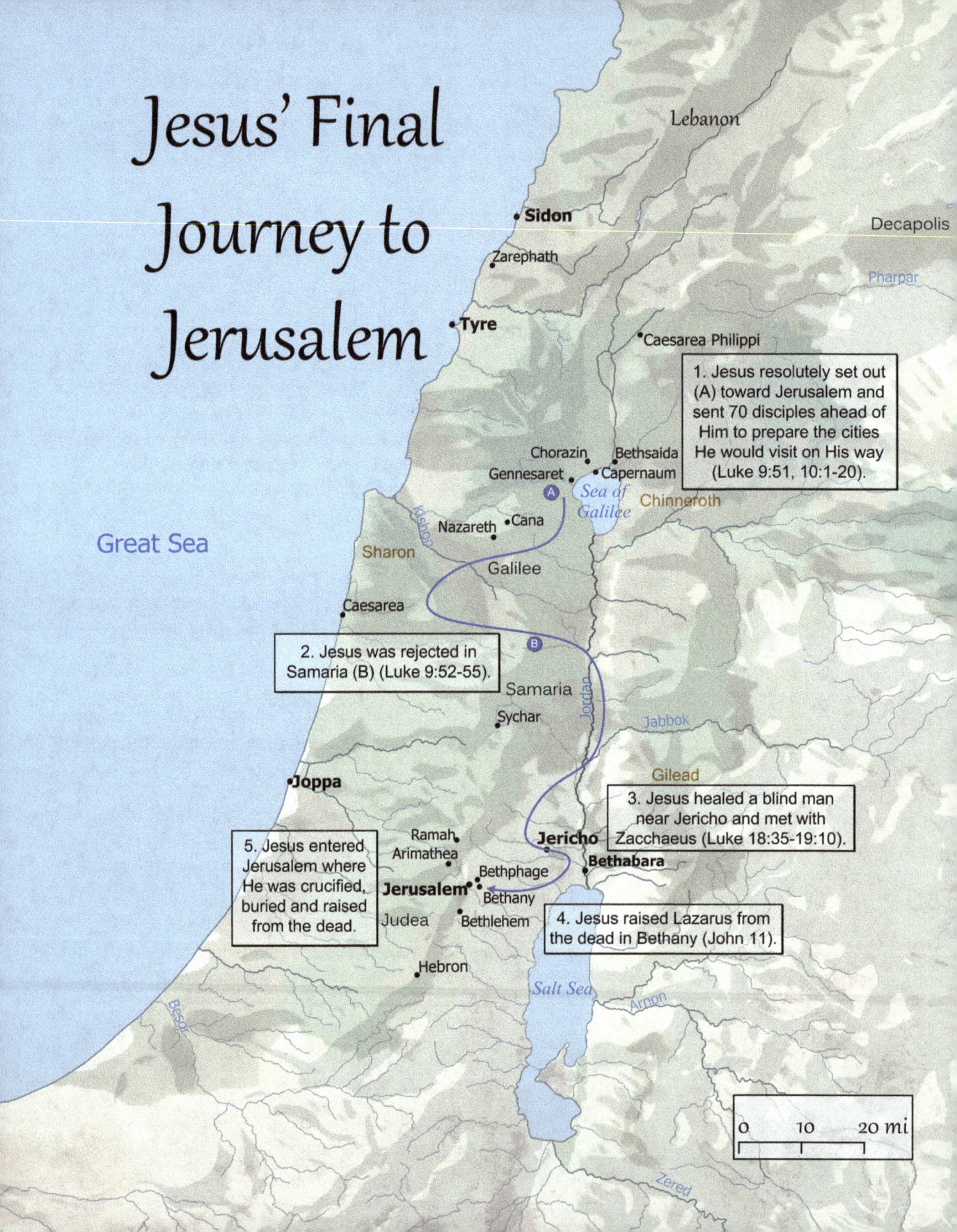

LESSON 5.1

The Sending of the Seventy and the Fall of Satan

UNIT 5

THE STORY

Lesson Theme - Israel's final chance

Since His disciples had begun imitating Him, Jesus had been training them as they followed Him throughout the land of Israel. Several months before the events of this lesson, Jesus had sent out the twelve. That was more than just training; the twelve disciples had actually carried out the ministry of Jesus. If that was the case with the twelve, it was even more true with the seventy. Jesus had set out resolutely toward Jerusalem—knowing that He was heading toward His death (Luke 9:51). In this lesson, Jesus sent out seventy disciples into all of the villages and towns that He was about to go through; this was the last chance these towns had to believe the gospel of the kingdom and trust in Jesus.

As Jesus was approaching Jerusalem, He sent messengers ahead of Him to prepare a Samaritan village for the coming of the Messiah (Luke 9:52). The people of this village didn't welcome Jesus because He was heading toward Jerusalem (the Samaritans worshiped in a different location and wanted Jesus to be *their* Messiah). In response, James and John (the Sons of Thunder) asked Jesus if they should call down fire from heaven to destroy that city, but Jesus rebuked them (Luke 9:54-55).

It is tempting to think that James and John simply didn't get Jesus' mission, but it is really more complicated than that. In the parable of the wheat and the tares, Jesus said that at the end of the age "angels" would go throughout the field (Israel) and separate between wheat and tares. The tares would be burned in a fire (Matt

OVERVIEW

Jesus set His face resolutely toward Jerusalem; He was going there to die. As He made His way throughout the land and even into Gentile territories, He sent out seventy of His disciples to announce His coming and give the people a final chance to repent. This was to fulfill the parable of the wheat and tares. His disciples returned with joy because they had power over demons. Jesus rejoiced with them, for their victory wasn't just earthly; He saw Satan fall from heaven. He validated His disciples' excitement, but told them to take the most joy in the fact that their names were recorded in heaven.

SOURCE MATERIAL

Luke 9:51-10:24

13:24-30, 36-42). And here they were at the end of the age; Jesus was on the way to Jerusalem to bring in a new age through His resurrection. Furthermore, the Greek word "angel" simply means messenger and is the same word used in Luke 8:52 translated as "messengers." The end of the age had come; messengers were being sent out to find weeds. What's next in the parable? Fire. What James and John were doing actually represents a pretty good grasp on the parable; they were just off on the timing a bit. Before the earthly judgement, there had to be a spiritual judgement in the heavenly realms.

Unit 5: Jesus' Final Days

OBJECTIVES

Feel...

- excited along with the disciples about the power given to us by Jesus Christ.
- even more excited that Jesus called us His family.
- an anticipation of the approaching end of Jesus' ministry.

Understand...

- why James and John wanted to call down fire from heaven on the Samaritan village.
- that although Jesus rebuked James and John, they weren't far from the truth.
- that this was the last chance for individuals and cities of Israel to repent before the end of Jesus' ministry.
- that the seventy Jesus sent out were the "angels" sent out in the parable of the wheat and the tares; they were assigning judgment to towns that rejected Jesus.
- the significance of Satan falling on account of the work of the seventy.
- that we are given the ongoing task of crushing the head of the serpent.
- the significance of the numbers twelve and seventy.

Apply this understanding by...

- living into your calling to exercise great power over evil on the earth.
- being ever joyful that we are a part of the family of Christ.

It was now coming down to the end of Jesus' ministry, and the stakes were really high. Cities that had rejected Him up to this point were hearing from Jesus for the last time. Those who wanted to follow Jesus and the disciples would have to follow now; in a short time He would be gone and wouldn't pass through their city again. In Luke 9:57-62, Jesus talked to three would-be disciples, each with their own barrier to following Him. The first thought he was willing to follow Jesus *anywhere*, but Jesus warned that He had no home. The second wanted to bury his father, but Jesus commanded him to "Let the dead bury their own dead" (Luke 9:60). The third simply wanted to go say goodbye to his family, but Jesus said that if he looked back after he began, he wasn't fit for service in the kingdom.

These three interactions with would-be disciples take us back to the parable of the sower (Matt 13:1-23). These potential followers were like the seeds choked out by thorns or the ones with shallow roots in the rocky soil. They *wanted* to follow Jesus, but they wanted to do it in their time and on their terms; it mattered not how noble their task was; the time to follow Jesus was now. The same was true for individuals as was true for cities of Israel; this was Jesus' last time through Israel and might be their last chance to follow Him.

Next, Jesus sent out seventy disciples to prepare areas of Israel for His coming, just like He did a few verses before with the two who went ahead of Him into the Samaritan village and much like He had done a few months earlier when He sent out the twelve. Again, Jesus alluded back to the parable of the wheat and tares: "The harvest truly is great, but the laborers are few; therefore pray the Lord of the harvest to send out laborers into His harvest. Go your way; behold, I send you out as lambs among wolves" (Luke 10:2-3, cf Matt 13:30).

Again, the disciples were the harvesters and were sent out as messengers (angels). Their task was twofold. First, they were harvesting wheat—they were preaching the gospel of the kingdom and setting aside for the kingdom any person or village who trusted in the Lord. Second, they were setting aside tares for destruction. Those towns that rejected them were to get the following speech, "The very dust of your city which clings to us we wipe off against you. Nevertheless know this, that the kingdom of God has come near you" (Luke 10:11). Jesus added, "It will be more bearable on that day for Sodom than for that town" (Luke 10:12, NIV).

Returning to James' and John's response to the rejection Jesus received in the Samaritan village, we see how right they really were. The towns that rejected Jesus would receive a fire from heaven type of judgement, but not until the appointed judgement day. James' and John's timing was off. The battle they were fighting was first a heavenly/spiritual battle and secondarily a battle for the world. There would come a day in the not too distant future when God would bring destruction on these cities (A.D. 70 and the revolts in the following years), but for now the battle was in the angelic realm.

The disciples returned from their mission and reported to Jesus with joy that "even the demons are subject to us in Your name" (Luke 10:17). They had experienced profound success in their mission; but their success was even more profound than they thought. Jesus told them, "I saw Satan fall like lightning from heaven" (Luke 10:18). They didn't just gain an earthly victory, they were making war on Satan. Before God would bring judgement on the cities of earth, He was bringing judgement on the serpent. Jesus was the ultimate head-crusher (Gen 3:15); in a short time, He would defeat the serpent on the cross, but the disciples were given the opportunity to participate in that defeat.

The disciples were head-crushers too; they had already seen success in that, but their task was not finished. Jesus told them in Luke 10:19, "I give you the authority to trample on serpents and scorpions, and over all the power of the enemy, and nothing shall by any means hurt you." How exciting it must have been for the disciples to be given that power! But Jesus gave them (and us) something even better; we are part of His family; "Nevertheless do not rejoice in this, that the spirits are subject to you, but rather rejoice because your names are written in heaven" (Luke 10:20).

In response to seeing His disciples experience this kind of success against the enemy, Jesus "rejoiced in the Spirit" (Luke 10:21). Jesus was the ultimate head-crusher, but He was not just here to get the job done. He came to create a new people, the body of Christ who would stay on earth as a head-crushing people after He ascended. Jesus' ultimate victory was not His defeat of the serpent, but His redemption of the people the serpent was seeking to devour and His turning them back against the serpent to defeat him. This prospect brought Jesus great joy, and He praised the Father for it.

APPLICATION

As apostles of Jesus, we are given incredible powers in the world and called to use them. Christians are not just *regular people*; we are called to crush the head of the serpent. This is a phenomenal calling, and if you aren't living into it, it's time to take the next step. BUT, being a Christian is not just about crushing the serpent's head; it's about being in God's family. That is what we should really be excited about (Luke 9:18-20).

Unit 5: Jesus' Final Days

ADDITIONAL NOTES

Jesus had sent out the twelve on one occasion and the seventy on another occasion. These numbers are a clue to how Jesus' mission to the world would work out. The twelve were sent *only* to the lost sheep of Israel. The twelve represent the twelve tribes of Israel, and the gospel went first to them. The seventy were sent ahead of Jesus; we aren't told where all they went, but they weren't prohibited from going to the Gentiles. We know that before Jesus went to Jerusalem, He passed through the region of Tyre and Sidon and the Decapolis as well. In all likelihood, the seventy went ahead of Jesus into these Gentile regions. In Genesis 10-11, seventy nations are recorded as nations that settled the world after the flood. This became something of a symbolic number; seventy represents the nations of the Gentiles. And ultimately, the gospel would go out to the rest of the world.

ACTIVITIES

1. Write a Short Story. In the space provided below, write a short story from the perspective of one of the seventy disciples whom Jesus sent out. Include the disciples' experience in one of the towns they visited. The story should also convey the joy and excitement the disciples felt at the success of their mission. _____

Lesson 5.1

EVALUATION

1. Why would James and John think it was a good idea to call down fire on the Samaritan village? Why were they wrong? _____

2. Why did Jesus send the seventy through Israel at this point? _____

3. Why would the success of the seventy cause Satan to fall from heaven? _____

4. What are we called to do in the world? _____

5. What is significant about Jesus sending His disciples out twice? _____

   Related to this, what is the significance of the numbers twelve and seventy? _____

LESSON 5.2

Jesus Raised Lazarus from the Dead

UNIT 5

THE STORY

Lesson Theme - Jesus demonstrated that He and the Father are one by raising Lazarus from the dead, exciting both His follower and His adversaries.

In Matthew 12, when the religious leaders rejected Jesus, they asked Him for a sign. Of course, He didn't give them a sign on that occasion because they had just attributed His previous sign to the power of Beelzebub. He did, however, promise them another sign, the sign of Jonah. The sign of Jonah meant that Jesus would spend three days and three nights in the "belly" of the earth, just as Jonah spent three days and three nights in the belly of the fish (Matt 12:40). For the religious leaders, the raising of Lazarus, who had been buried for three days, was a preview of His own resurrection, His own sign of Jonah. But for His disciples, the sign was meant to strengthen their faith and show them the glory of God.

Jesus had stated on a number of occasions that He would be crucified and raised from the dead, but His disciples still didn't get it. They didn't get it because they didn't get the principle of baptism: death precedes resurrection; suffering precedes glory. And ultimately, in resurrection, the glory of God is most marvelously displayed.

The story of Lazarus occurs shortly before Jesus came to Jerusalem for the Passover at which He would be crucified. It was reported to Jesus that Lazarus was sick in the town of Bethany where he and his sisters Mary and Martha lived (John 11:1). Traveling to Bethany would take Jesus very close to Jerusalem where it was dangerous

OVERVIEW

To the disciples' consternation, Jesus headed to Judea a couple of days after He heard that His friend Lazarus was dead. The disciples were concerned that Jesus could get Himself killed in Judea. When He arrived in Bethany, Lazarus was already dead. Martha, Lazarus' sister, really wanted Jesus to raise him from the dead. Jesus assured her that *He* was the resurrection and the life, but stopped short of clearly saying that He was going to raise Lazarus from the dead. Jesus then met with Mary and joined in her mourning. When they arrived at the tomb, Jesus called Lazarus out, and he came. Many were in awe at this miracle, but some reported it to the religious leaders in Jerusalem who plotted all the more to kill Jesus.

SOURCE MATERIAL

- **John 11:1-54**
- Luke 10:38-42
- Psalm 16:10

for Him to be. When He heard that his friend Lazarus was sick, Jesus said, "This sickness will not end in death. No, it is for God's glory so that God's Son may be glorified through it" (John 11:4, NIV). Of course, Lazarus did die, but the story doesn't *end* that way. Without a doubt, Jesus' disciples took this statement to mean that Lazarus *wouldn't* die; instead, Jesus meant to give them a first hand look at a death and resurrection story.

Unit 5: Jesus' Final Days

OBJECTIVES

Feel...

- Martha's frustration at Jesus' ambiguity.
- sad with Mary and Jesus at the loss of Lazarus.
- awe at the power of Jesus to raise Lazarus.

Understand...

- that the raising of Lazarus was a preview of Jesus' own resurrection and an aspect of the sign of Jonah.
- that the disciples still didn't get that Jesus was going to die.
- what Jesus meant when He said, "This sickness will not end in death."
- that Jesus intentionally waited until Lazarus had died before He headed to Bethany—He was using this as an occasion to display God's glory.
- that Martha was asking Jesus to raise Lazarus from the dead.
- that Jesus didn't give Martha a clear answer, but pointed her to His identity as the resurrection and the life.
- that Jesus felt Mary's pain.
- that there was no stench in the tomb because Jesus had prayed that the Father would preserve Lazarus—this was a sign that Jesus and the Father are one.
- that Jesus' raising Lazarus from the dead excited His followers and antagonized His adversaries.

Apply this understanding by...

- believing that there is no problem too difficult for Jesus.

A couple of days after hearing about Lazarus' sickness, Jesus told His disciples that it was time to go to Judea (John 11:6-7). They knew that His life would be in danger if He got near Jerusalem, so they objected. Of course, Jesus wasn't worried; He knew He was headed for His time of suffering and that it was all going to go according to the Father's plan. The disciples though, were living in fear that something bad might happen to their master. Jesus' somewhat cryptic statement in John 11:9-10 was His way of telling the disciples that they didn't need to worry about what was going to happen; they were walking with the light of the world while the religious leaders in Jerusalem were stumbling around in the darkness. In fact, they had the light *in them*, and the darkness could never take that away. This didn't particularly give the disciples assurance that nothing bad was going to happen; rather, it called them to a place of rest and trust in the Messiah and the Father's plan.

Speaking cryptically again, Jesus told the disciples that Lazarus "sleeps," and He was going to "wake him up" (John 11:11). Jesus meant the sleep of death, but the disciples thought that Lazarus was finally getting a little rest, and therefore would be on the mend soon.

At this point, Jesus decided it was time to just speak plainly and told the disciples that Lazarus was dead (John 11:14). Jesus probably could've made it back to Judea in time to heal Lazarus before he died; but instead, He had waited two days where they were. Jesus wanted Lazarus to die so that He could raise him. This was mostly for the benefit of His disciples so that they could see the glory of God and believe. The disciples reluctantly followed the Lord to Bethany, knowing that there was a good chance He would die in Judea (John 11:16).

Lazarus had two sisters, Mary and Martha. In Luke 10 we get a glimpse into the character of these two women. When Jesus had entered a city (probably Bethany), Martha greeted Him and invited Him to her house. Martha busied herself with much serving while her sister Mary simply sat at Jesus' feet and listened to Him speak. When Martha complained that Mary had left all the work to her, Jesus said that Mary had chosen the good part and that would not be taken away from her. Martha was a worker; she got things done. Mary lived in the moment; some things wouldn't get done, but she wouldn't miss the most important thing.

In the story of Lazurus' death, we again see a contrast with Mary and Martha. When Jesus arrived in town, Martha hurried to meet Him and said, "Lord, if You had been here, my brother would not have died" (John 11:21). She then hastened to add, "But even now I know that whatever You ask of God, God will give You" (John 11:22). In essence, Martha was saying, "You should've been here sooner, but it's not too late." Martha believed that Jesus could raise her brother from the dead and was asking Him to do that. As before, Martha was getting things done while Mary remained at home in mourning.

The exchange between Jesus and Martha following this is interesting. Jesus certainly understood that Martha was implying He should raise Lazarus from the dead. He was already planning on doing it and certainly wouldn't have missed the hint. So when He responded, "Your brother will rise again" (John 11:23), we need to ask: was He talking about the last day, or the resurrection He was about to bring about? The answer is almost certainly both. Jesus was in the business of bringing the future of the resurrection into the present. In fact, His own resurrection was an advance payment on the coming new creation.

But Martha didn't get it; she thought that Jesus was simply talking about the future resurrection. We can almost hear a bit of exasperation in her voice, "I know he will rise again in the resurrection *at the last day*" (John 11:24, emphasis added). She was not interested in the theology of the last day right now; she wanted Jesus to raise Lazarus today. She was trying to get things done.

Jesus, however, was interested in the theology of the last day, because He was about ready to bring it to life. Jesus, *presently*, is the resurrection and the life (John 11:25). This means that anyone who trusts in Jesus will both live forever and will be resurrected once they die. The implication for Martha was that there was nothing to stop Jesus from answering her request to raise Lazarus from the dead. Jesus asked if she believed what He had just told her: that He is the resurrection and the life. She responded in the affirmative, clarifying that she understood that He could do this because He was the Messiah, the Son of God who was coming into the world (John 11:27).

At this point, John cuts away from the conversation with Martha, and we are left to wonder if she really got it—that Jesus was about to raise Lazarus from the dead. Jesus apparently directed her to get Mary, who came to Jesus weeping.

Mary approached Jesus by saying nearly exactly the same thing Martha had, "Lord, if you had been here, my brother would not have died" (John 11:32). But while Martha had gone on to imply that Jesus should raise Lazarus, Mary stopped there. Martha hadn't allowed herself to enter into mourning on the bet that Jesus would raise her brother from the dead. Mary, again, was living in the moment. Her brother had died. She wept. So did Jesus (John 11:35).

Unit 5: Jesus' Final Days

When they arrived at the tomb, Jesus asked for the stone to be rolled away (John 11:39). Martha objected on account of the odor of the body. Lazarus had been in the grave for four days, meaning that his body would be well into the process of decay. We still don't know whether Martha ever understood that Jesus was going to raise Lazarus. Her statement here seems to indicate that at least she was on the fence. Jesus responded to her objection by pointing her back to faith, "Did I not say to you that if you would believe you would see the glory of God?" (John 11:40).

John gives us a riddle at this point. After they rolled the stone away, Jesus looked toward heaven and said, "Father, I thank You that You have heard Me" (John 11:41). John intends for us to ask, "What did Jesus pray to the Father?" Jesus hadn't yet raised Lazarus from the dead, so that couldn't be what He was referring to. But it must've been something that everyone there could have perceived because Jesus said that the reason He thanked the Father was so that "they may believe that You sent me" (John 11:42).

So what could possibly validate that Jesus was sent by the Father? *There was no stench.* This seems to be the only possible explanation. Martha had reminded the entire crowd that there would be a terrible stench, but when they moved the stone away, Jesus looked up and said, "Thanks, Dad," so everyone would know that the reason it didn't stink was because Jesus had asked the Father ahead of time to preserve Lazarus' body.

The effect of this miracle was that it took the focus off of Jesus alone and brought glory to the Father as well. The glorification of the Father glorified the Son because it demonstrated that He was acting on the authority of the Father when He raised Lazarus. But notice that Jesus didn't ask the Father to raise Lazarus—He commanded Lazarus to come out (John 11:43). Jesus *is* the resurrection and the life. He was acting in accordance with the Father, but the Father had given Him real power over death.

Jesus had told His disciples that Lazarus' sickness would not end in death, and now His disciples saw what He meant. Lazarus' story didn't end in death, but that didn't mean that death didn't come along the way. Jesus wanted to drive home the lesson He had been teaching His disciples for quite some time: the path to glory goes through death, suffering and trial. He wanted this narrative of death and resurrection to get into their bones so that they too would live that way. In truth, they wouldn't really get it until they saw Jesus raised from the dead, an event which was not far in the offing.

In many ways, Lazarus' death and resurrection is a prefigurement of Jesus' death and resurrection. Jesus had prayed that though Lazarus had been in the grave for four days, his body would not suffer decay. Likewise, the Father would not allow Jesus to see corruption in the grave (Ps 16:10) and raise Him after three days. Of course, Lazarus would die again, while Jesus was raised to an eternal resurrection.

John draws our attention to the reaction that this miracle received. When Jesus wept with Mary, some were impressed with His love while others wondered why He didn't prevent Lazarus from dying (John 11:36-37). Following the raising of Lazarus, many believed in Jesus, but some reported this miracle to the religious leaders who began plotting to kill Jesus (John 11:45-47).

Why was this miracle such a threat to the religious establishment? If Jesus continued to do things like this, they argued, everyone would believe in Him and a revolt would be started. Inevitably, this would bring a fierce response from the Romans who would come in and take away, in the words of the religious leaders, "*our* temple and *our* nation" (John 11:48, NIV, emphasis added). They were completely blind to what God might be up to and were only concerned about maintaining their respectable religious establishment.

In a moment of prophetic insight, the high priest, Caiaphas, said, "It is better for you that one man die for the people than that the whole nation perish" (John 11:50, NIV). The religious leaders thought that by killing Jesus they were saving Israel from the judgment of the Romans. But in reality, Jesus' death would save Israel from their sins. The judgement from the Romans would still come, but all who believed in Jesus would be saved.

With this line of reasoning, the religious leaders began plotting to kill Jesus (John 11:53). But, hey, if you're going to get in trouble for something, it might as well be raising someone from the dead. Shortly hereafter, Jesus would enter Jerusalem amidst a combination of high praise from the crowds of people who had heard of His greatness and an official plot to try, convict and kill Him.

APPLICATION

The application here is a "believe" application, not a "do" application. Jesus heard the Father's voice and obeyed Him. Jesus prayed that God would preserve Lazarus in the grave, and God did it. He and the Father are one. Jesus raised Lazarus from the dead; what can He not do? What sin in your life is too strong for Jesus to overcome? What hardship is too difficult for Jesus to heal? Believe in Jesus!

ACTIVITIES

1. Journal Time. Think of a struggle you're going through, a sin you feel is impossible to overcome, etc. In the space below, write a prayer asking God to increase your faith in His ability to heal and overcome. _____

_____

_____

_____

_____

_____

_____

_____

Unit 5: Jesus' Final Days

2. Draw Lazarus. In the space provided below, draw a picture of Lazarus coming out of the grave still wrapped in his grave clothes (or perhaps in the process of unwrapping them). You can include additional details if you would like such as the open tomb, Jesus and the crowds, etc.

Lesson 5.2

EVALUATION

1. What did Jesus mean when He said, "This sickness will not end in death" (John 11:4)? _____

2. Why did Jesus wait until Lazarus had died before He went to Bethany? _____

3. Why was Martha so eager to approach Jesus and say that she knew God would do anything He asked? _____

4. How did Jesus respond to Martha's pressing request? _____

5. What did Jesus do when He saw Mary's pain at the loss of her brother? _____

6. Everyone was expecting there to be a stench after the stone was rolled away from Lazarus' tomb; how do we know that there wasn't a smell? _____

7. What was the effect of Jesus thanking the Father that there was no stench? _____

8. What kind of response did Jesus' raising of Lazarus provoke? _____

LESSON 5.3

Jesus' Arrival in Jerusalem

THE STORY

Lesson Theme - Jesus entered Jerusalem in glory and was challenged by the authorities.
There are a number of things that go on in this lesson, but the focus is on the contrast of Jesus' triumphal entry (the response of the people) and the rapidly escalating conflict with the religious leaders.

Jesus *is* King. He didn't need the validation of the religious leaders to make that true. He sought their validation, and since He was their King, they should have proclaimed that truth with all the authority of their position. But when the religious leaders rejected Jesus, they rejected their King; they *did not* simply reject a man who wanted to be king.

Jesus was aware of where He was in the Story. Israel had been waiting for a king for generations. They had sought deliverance from the kingdoms that had controlled them, many times to the point of bloodshed. Their prophets longed for and wrote about the King who was to come. One of these prophecies, recorded in Zechariah 9:9, foretells that the Messiah would ride victoriously into Jerusalem on a donkey.

To modern ears, a donkey doesn't sound like the transportation of a king, but in ancient Israel it was. A horse was an animal of war, but a donkey was a sign of peace. Jesus entered Jerusalem peacefully, but also with a sharp message. He was announcing that He was the King of Peace; He knew the established authorities wouldn't take this message well. The crowds understood

OVERVIEW

Jesus entered Jerusalem triumphantly on a donkey, as a king victorious on the battlefield, returning to sit on His throne. But instead of going to a palace, He went to the temple where He was challenged by the religious leaders of Israel. He easily answered their questions and turned their attempted traps back on them. Jesus rebuked the leaders of Israel and cried for the loss of His city.

SOURCE MATERIAL

- **Matthew 21:1-23:39**
- Mark 11:1-12:40

Jesus' message of peace and kingly authority and responded by hailing Him as King. Their praise drew on Jesus' identity as the Son of David and a selection from Psalm 118:25-26, extolling the victorious Messiah.

Jesus' arrival in Jerusalem portrays Him as the new David, the victorious conqueror who had just finished His victory and was returning to the capital city to take a seat on His throne and rule in peace over His kingdom. But the fulfillment was inverted. Instead of going to a palace, Jesus went to the temple. Instead of taking His seat on the throne, He made His way toward the cross.

Imagine how the disciples must've felt when Jesus rode into Jerusalem on a donkey to much

Unit 5: Jesus' Final Days

OBJECTIVES

Feel...

- the tension of Jesus riding victoriously, even though He knew He was heading to His death.
- the pain, love and anger Jesus felt as He rebuked the religious leaders.

Understand...

- the significance of Jesus riding into Jerusalem on a donkey.
- that the crowds got the message: Jesus riding in on a donkey was the act of a victorious conquering King coming to sit on His throne.
- that Jesus cleansed the temple, antagonizing His adversaries, but healed the hurting and broken.
- that the fig tree was symbolic of Israel.
- that the religious leaders approached Jesus, officially challenging His authority in anticipation of arresting Him.
- that the religious leaders tried to trap Jesus with tricky questions, but He actually trapped them.
- the general meaning of Jesus' parables: that the religious leaders had abdicated the responsibility God gave them and would be judged for it.
- that Jesus' annunciation of the woes against the religious leaders was out of a spirit of love and pain.

Apply this understanding by...

- thinking about the way Jesus talked to people and considering what it would look like in your life to imitate Jesus.

fanfare. They knew this story—the King was here and with Him, His kingdom. They were certainly in a state of high rejoicing and complete confidence that there was nothing bad in the future. The anticipation created by the triumphal entry undoubtedly contributed to their shock when Jesus was arrested, tried and crucified that very week. But Jesus didn't mind putting them through this period of disorientation. Actually, that experience of disorientation was the only way they would learn the deep truths about suffering and glory that Jesus had been teaching them. This next week was going to invert their entire world, and they would come out of it transformed. That's what the crucifixion and resurrection of Christ does to people.

The triumphal entry occurred on Sunday. After entering the city, Jesus went to the temple, but He didn't do much there that day. It was getting late, so He headed back to Bethany (where He was staying) for the night (Mark 11:11). On Monday, He returned to Jerusalem and drove out the money changers, turning over their tables and driving them out (Matt 21:11-13). He had done this before, but this time the tension was at an all time high; He was just asking to be arrested. But that was not all He did; He also healed the blind and lame (Matt 21:14-15). And this part is cool: the children who saw Him healing people *got it*; they understood the significance of the triumphal entry; they knew that Jesus was the Messiah, the Son of David, and so they shouted it out in the temple courts (Matt 21:15). The religious leaders *hated* this and approached Jesus about it. Quoting Psalm 8:2, Jesus asked, "Have you never read, 'Out of the mouth of babes and nursing infants You have perfected praise'?"(Matt 21:16). Jesus' response would have pushed the religious leaders to the boiling point, but that had never bothered Him before.

Lesson 5.3

On the way into the city that morning, Jesus had cursed a fruitless fig tree (Mark 11:12-14). The next morning, Jesus and His disciples found the fig tree withered, and the disciples were astonished (Mark 11:20-21; Matthew tells the story of the fig tree in one short narrative without explaining what happened on each day—Matt 21:18-22). Jesus cursed the fig tree because it was fruitless, and immediately, it withered. Like that fig tree, Israel was fruitless, especially the temple. Jesus' curse on the fig tree was symbolic of the curse of judgement He was bringing on Jerusalem.

On Tuesday, Jesus had His final clash with the religious leaders before His arrest. Notice that it was just two days after His triumphal entry as King. While Jesus was in the temple teaching, He was approached by the chief priests and elders—the top dogs. This was not just another round of verbal sparring between Jesus and the religious leaders, this was an official challenge to Jesus and their final attempt to get Him in line.

The question they asked Him was intended to be a trap, "By what authority are You doing these things?" (Matt 21:23). If Jesus said that He was operating on His own human authority, then He would undermine His entire ministry. If He said He was operating on the authority of God in heaven, then they, being the official religious leaders, could act against Him. Jesus' response entrapped the trappers. Instead of answering them, He asked whether John was operating by human or heavenly authority (Matt 21:24-25). They understood what He was doing (Matt 21:25b-26). If they said John's authority was from heaven, then they had to acknowledge Jesus' authority since John pointed to Jesus. If they said that John's authority was of human origin, then they would be castigated by the people. John was popular when he was alive, but now that he was a martyr, he enjoyed saintly status among the people. The religious leaders couldn't respond, and simply said, "We do not know" (Matt 21:27). Jesus' trap not only undermined their plan to arrest Him, it also forced them to essentially admit their incompetence to judge Jesus. If they couldn't figure out where John got his authority, why should they be trusted to make judgements on Jesus' claims?

Had Jesus simply responded to their question, He probably would've been arrested right then and there, but it was not yet His time. So He responded with three parables. These parables were clearly aimed at the religious leaders. In the first, the parable of the two sons (Matt 21:28-32), the first son represents the religious leaders who say they will obey but don't. The second son represents the tax collectors and prostitutes. They don't intend to obey, but when Jesus shows up, they do. In the parable of the tenants (Matt 21:33-46), God is the landowner, Israel is the vineyard, the religious leaders are the servants, the messengers are the prophets, and Jesus is the Son. Jesus' message to the religious leaders was clear: You killed the prophets and you even killed God's Son; your judgement is coming." The final parable is about Jesus taking away the kingdom offer to the leaders of Israel and inviting all who will come; it anticipates the gospel going to the nations (Matt 22:1-14).

Jesus didn't tell these parables to win the religious leaders over. The parables were a rebuke, but one Jesus knew would provoke them to anger. They immediately began making plans to trap Him (Matt 22:15). They *really* wanted to win a round. They came back with a series of questions to try to trick Jesus into saying something that would be cause for them to arrest Him or put Him in danger of being arrested by the Romans. In each case, Jesus answered both bib-

lically and shrewdly, amazing the crowds (Matt 22:22). After the Pharisees were done asking Him questions, Jesus asked them the question, "Whose Son is [the Christ]?" (Matt 22:42). Their answer, as expected, was that He was the Son of David. Jesus anticipated their answer and asked another question, "How then does David in the Spirit call Him 'Lord?'" (Matt 22:43), making reference to Psalm 110. Jesus continued, "If David calls Him 'Lord,' how can He be his son?" (Matt 22:45). The religious leaders' job was to protect Israel from false Messiahs *and* establish the authority of the true Messiah when He came, but they had decided beforehand that if someone claimed to be the Son of God then he was guilty of blasphemy and couldn't be the Messiah. By quoting Psalm 110, Jesus refuted them and proved that they didn't even know how to read the Bible. No one bothered to ask Jesus any more questions after that.

Matthew 23 contains some of Jesus' harshest words to the religious leaders. Pronouncing woe after woe upon them, and even engaging in name-calling, "Serpents, brood of vipers!" (Matt 23:33). It all sounds quite harsh, and it was, but notice how it ended. Jesus closed with these words, "O Jerusalem, Jerusalem, the one who kills the prophets and stones those who are sent to her! How often I wanted to gather your children together, as a hen gathers her chicks under *her* wings, but you were not willing!" (Matt 23:37). It is easy to imagine anger in Jesus' voice in the tirade that led up to these words, but this final paragraph is hard to read without imagining tears in His eyes. Jesus *really* wanted to save Jerusalem. He loved her, and she rejected Him. This helps us understand where Jesus was coming from in His previous harsh words. He was not angry because He hated the religious leaders; He was angry because He *loved* them.

APPLICATION

We often think of Jesus as gentle, meek and mild. But that is not at all the Jesus we see in this lesson. Jesus was bold, shrewd and discerning with His adversaries. There is a place for gracious and kind speech to your enemies, but there is also a place for harsh and bracing language toward those who have rejected God. Be honest with yourself though, you may very well not be mature enough to start speaking this way—it takes tremendous wisdom and a firm relationship with God—but this kind of rhetoric should be on your radar as something God may someday call you to.

ACTIVITIES

1. Dramatic Reading. Jesus really went after the Pharisees and teachers of the law in Matthew 23:13-39, but He was speaking out of love, out of the pain of loss. We often don't think of love and anger going together, but this was the way it was for Jesus. His love is especially evident in the last paragraph (Matthew 23:37-39). Here's your assignment: read this entire section out loud and with great drama. Increase the intensity of the anger up to verse 36, then really break down in tears and pain in the final paragraph. Seeing this transition will really help put Jesus' angry words into perspective. Following the reading, write your thoughts in the space provided on the following page.

Unit 5: Jesus' Final Days

Dramatic Reading (cont.) _____
_____
_____
_____
_____
_____

2. Understanding the Traps. Read one of the following passages, then answer the questions below.

Passages:

- Matthew 22:15-22
- Matthew 22:23-33
- Matthew 22:34-40

1. What were the religious leaders expecting Jesus to say in response to their question? _____
_____
_____
_____
_____

2. How could that question have trapped Jesus? _____
_____
_____
_____
_____

3. How did Jesus surprise them to undermine the trap? _____
_____
_____
_____
_____

Lesson 5.3

EVALUATION

1. What does it mean that Jesus rode into Jerusalem on a donkey? _____

2. How did the crowds respond to this? _____

3. What was the meaning of Jesus causing the fruitless fig tree to wither? _____

4. Jesus had had many clashes with the religious leaders. What was different about this clash? _____

5. How did Jesus respond to the question of the religious leaders who were attempting to trap Him?

6. What is the general meaning of the parables that Jesus directed to the religious leaders? _____

7. What was the main emotion behind Jesus' woes upon the Pharisees? _____

LESSON 5.4

Jesus Instituted Communion

UNIT 5

THE STORY

Lesson Theme - Jesus interpreted and transformed the Passover into a ritual meal commemorating His death.

Adam and Eve were freely permitted to eat from every tree in the garden except the tree of the knowledge of good and evil. The tree of life was a sacramental tree and by eating it they communed with God. God later delivered Israel from slavery in Egypt through the Passover meal, in which a sacrificial animal became a substitute for the firstborn. The people ate the sacrificial animal as an act of communion with and gratitude toward God. Throughout their history, Israel celebrated the Passover as an act of communion and memorial. Furthermore, they regularly offered a sacrifice called the peace offering at the temple that taught a similar lesson: the sacrificial animal became a fellowship meal with God. In this lesson, Jesus institutes the Lord's table, the communion meal which all these previous communion meals had been foreshadowing.

Jesus collided with the religious leaders in the temple on Tuesday of Passover week. We know that He was teaching daily in the temple, and so on Wednesday He was probably also there, teaching and healing people, but no specifics are recorded in the gospels. The next recorded events happened on Thursday. Thursday is the day the Passover meal was eaten, and so it was considered a significant day by the Jews. Of course, it was a significant day for Jesus as well. But He didn't spend it battling the Pharisees or healing people in the crowds. That time had

OVERVIEW

Jesus' final time of fellowship with His disciples was the Passover meal, a meal with a rich history of communion with God. Jesus transformed that meal from a memorial of the exodus to a memorial of God's deliverance through Jesus Christ. When we partake of communion, we are feasting with God and enjoying the blessing of the future in the midst of our present wandering.

SOURCE MATERIAL

- **Luke 22:3-20**
- Matthew 26:14-29
- Mark 14:10-25
- John 13-17

come and gone. Jesus spent His last day with His disciples, His closest twelve.

On that day, Jesus sent Peter and John ahead to prepare for the Passover meal (Luke 22:8). Jesus and His disciples didn't live in Jerusalem, so they needed a place to celebrate. Nothing was accidental; Jesus told them where to go and how to find the room that the Father had provided for them to celebrate the meal. John and Peter went and found it just as Jesus had said (Luke 22:13).

When the time came for the meal, Jesus and all His disciples met in that upper guest room. John records the events of the evening in the most detail, while the other three gospels focus

31

Unit 5: Jesus' Final Days

OBJECTIVES

Feel...

- thankful that God invites us to eat a meal with Him.

Understand...

- the relationship between the tree of life, Passover, the peace offering and communion as sacramental meals.
- that the institution of communion is a transformation of Passover.
- the meaning of bread.
- the meaning of wine.
- the significance of eating Jesus' flesh and blood.
- that communion is a celebratory meal with God.

Apply this understanding by...

- approaching communion with reverence but joy as he eats with God.

---

in on Jesus instituting the communion meal. Interestingly, John leaves this part out. Like the gospels of Matthew, Mark and Luke, this lesson is going to focus in on the communion meal, but you'll also want to draw from John's gospel to get a sense of the general series of events that occurred in the upper room that evening.

When Jesus arrived in the upper room with His disciples, He washed their feet; then they moved into the meal setting. He warned Peter that he would deny Him three times and warned the disciples that one of them would betray him. Jesus sent Judas on his way, initiating the series of events that would lead to His crucifixion. After Judas left, Jesus and the eleven disciples ate the meal, Jesus instituted communion, and He spent the evening teaching them. In John there is a long discourse recorded in chapters 13-17 that communicates the content of what Jesus taught; in short, He was preparing the disciples for His departure and assuring them that they would be taken care of. After His teaching, they left the upper room and made their way across town to the Mount of Olives to pray.

Our main interest in this lesson is the actual institution of the communion meal. This is recorded in Luke 22:14-20. The traditional Passover feast consisted of a very specific sequence of events throughout this ritual meal, all meant to call the minds of the people back to the Passover lamb that delivered them out of Egypt. Jesus took this meal and transformed it. He is the *new* Passover meal. Historically, Jesus was making a staggering claim: "The deliverance I bring is bigger than the original Passover; in fact, the original Passover was just a precursor, a shadow of the deliverance I bring."

Jesus claimed to be bringing a second covenant. Moses brought the first covenant, inaugurated with a Passover meal. Jesus instituted the New Covenant with His own blood. In the first Passover, the sacrificial lamb was the important part. The lamb provided both the meat for the meal and the blood for the doorposts. In this Passover, Jesus didn't take a piece of meat and say, "I am the new Passover; eat this in remembrance of Me," because Jesus would be the last sacrifice. We no longer need to kill an animal to have peace and communion with God. Jesus told us that the bread is His flesh and the cup is His blood (John 6:56).

This brings us to the meaning of the communion meal. Jesus told us it is His memorial (Luke 22:19); and in biblical terms, His memorial is not only a way for us to remember Him, but also

a reminder to God of what Jesus did for us, a reminder to God that we partake of Christ's body and blood, that we are what we eat. Theology tells us that God needs no reminders, and as far as it goes, this is true. Jesus, however, told us to remind God regularly. "Why?" we want to know. Perhaps it is the same reason that we are to pray without ceasing—even though God knows our requests before we ask. Or perhaps it is for other reasons. The most pressing thing, however, is not to know why, but to obey God's command.

This is one of the necessary lessons of worship that must spill over into the world: the mysteries are many, our understanding is weak, and we obey in spite of it all. Not because we understand, but because we trust the God who guides us. In that trust God answers our prayer: "Thy will be done, on earth as it is in heaven."

Christ is our Passover, and in the communion meal, we eat and drink the ultimate Passover feast. Or maybe not quite the ultimate. One of the lessons of Passover and of communion, is that we are pilgrims in this world. But there's a right way and a wrong way to be a pilgrim.

If we think of ourselves as pilgrims in the sense that we're traveling from one *place* to another—now we're here on earth, but we're on our way to our home in heaven—then we won't necessarily care about the place that we're leaving behind. But this is exactly the wrong way to be a pilgrim.

You see, we are pilgrims in time. Heaven is important, but it's not the end of the world. We wait for the coming of Christ's kingdom, and then what a feast we will have! It will be the ultimate feast of the Lord's table, with Christ Himself drinking the cup with us in His Father's kingdom. That kingdom will not be in a far-off heaven, but right here on earth—the very same earth we are commanded to cultivate and protect.

Therefore, we live not as pilgrims who are going away, but as pilgrims who are waiting for this world to be turned into our home. This is the good news that we carry out to our neighbors: this world and its lusts are passing away. Stand apart from it, and seek the kingdom of God. Christ died for us so that we need not fall in love with the temporary world that is passing away; He has freed us to seek a home in His eternal kingdom that is coming to this earth.

Along with the meaning of the Lord's table as a whole, we need to consider the meaning of the elements. When we consider the question of what bread means, we face constant temptation to sidetrack the question into areas that are more comfortable:

> "What does bread mean to me?"—a question of individual emotional association.
>
> "What does bread symbolize in the Bible?"—an important part of the question, but we can't stop with the academic question or we'll miss the whole point.

We live in a meaningful world. Everything means something; everything is a message from a loving, majestic Triune God. Only when we begin to ask what each thing means do we begin to understand the world and our place in it. So what we're asking is what bread means in the world itself. When you see a loaf of bread sitting on the counter in your own kitchen, what does it mean? The Bible does speak about the meaning of bread, not just because bread symbolizes something in God's word, but because bread symbolizes something in God's world—the only world there is.

Bread is provision, it is blessing, it is strength. It is the product of dominion, a cooperation between God's blessing of the crops and man's labor in the fields, the mill and the bakery. Every loaf of bread is God's kindness, a demonstration of the image of God, of God's will being done on earth as it is in heaven, and when we eat this blessing, we receive strength. And so, of necessity, every loaf of bread is also a call to thank God.

As with bread, we are tempted to impose our own personal meaning on wine. Wine means excess and wild parties and losing control; wine means being beaten by your drunk father; wine means scandal and appearing like a sinner; whatever. Our personal associations are real, but they are not what wine *means*.

Wine means what God says it means. Lack of wine is either a form of fasting or a curse from God. God says wine is our labor blessed by His hand—which is to say it is the result of man having dominion over the earth, which is fulfilling his role as the image of God. It is God's blessing. It is the gift with which Jesus blessed a wedding; the drink served by Lady Wisdom in Solomon's Proverbs; part of the ascension offering lifted to God in the morning and evening sacrifices; the drink that Melchizedek, the royal priest, brought to Abraham; and the drink that Christ serves to Abraham's children by faith at His table. Wine is rejoicing and fellowship.

As with any blessing, wine can be abused, and Scripture is filled with warnings about that; it is a wicked mind that turns God's blessing into an occasion for sin. It's an equally wicked, pinched, joyless mind that thinks rejecting God's good gift is a holy thing to do. Both of these sins stem from a lack of gratitude.

APPLICATION

What you want to get out of this lesson is a fresh approach to the Lord's table at your church. Many churches present the Lord's table as simply an opportunity to confess sins and think about how bad you've been and how much you need Jesus. This is okay as far as it goes, but not nearly enough. In communion, *God is inviting you to a feast*; it's not just an object lesson, it's a meal with God.

ACTIVITIES

1. With a Smile On. Answer the following questions about how your church does communion.

Is it presented as a happy or sad event? _____

_____

_____

_____

Unit 5: Jesus' Final Days

What kind of music is played before, during and after? _____
_____
_____

What kind of behavior is expected during communion? (examples are bowing your head, meditating on your sins, singing, clapping hands, etc.) _____
_____
_____

We don't want you to be critical of your church, but we do want you to be aware of the attitude you have about the Lord's table. Next time your church does communion, think consciously about communion as a meal with the Lord. As you partake of it, thank the Lord, smile as though you are at a feast with friends and raise your head up, even if you need to keep your eyes closed. After doing these things at a communion service, write two to three sentences in response to the following question.

How did your joyful attitude change your experience of communion? _____
_____
_____
_____
_____
_____

2. The Meaning of Bread. Bread is an ancient food staple with a rich history and symbolism. Use the Internet or other resources you may have to research the history and symbolism of bread. Remember, the Internet can have some very helpful information, but don't believe everything you read there! Write a few sentences about what you found on the history of bread. _____
_____
_____
_____
_____

Lesson 5.4

Write a few sentences on the possible symbolism or meaning of bread.

What might have been some of the reasons why Jesus chose bread to be His body in the communion meal?

EVALUATION

1. What do the tree of life, Passover, the peace offering and communion all have in common?

2. How is communion related to Passover?

3. What is the meaning of bread in the world?

4. What is the meaning of wine in the world?

5. Why would Jesus want us to eat His flesh and drink His blood?

LESSON 5.5

Jesus Betrayed, Arrested and Forsaken

UNIT 5

THE STORY

Lesson Theme - Jesus willingly suffered betrayal, arrest, and abandonment.

Following the Passover meal, Jesus made His way across the city to the Mount of Olives. He knew *exactly* what was happening; His time had come. It was Jesus who sent Judas out to betray Him. Jesus went to the garden of Gethsemane to pray in preparation for this moment (Matt 26:36). Jesus willingly offered Himself to His enemies to be put to death and suffer abandonment by His closest followers. He knew that the time had come for His great promotion. As you study this lesson, don't forget that He knew what was coming — everything He did, He did calmly in the face of certain death by torture. It had come time for Jesus to obey the Father to the fullest.

Night fell and Jesus prayed in the garden of Gethsemane with His disciples. It was noted above that Jesus faced His calling calmly and obediently, but not without some serious preparation through prayer. Here we get a glimpse into what it felt like to be up against the task Jesus had before Him. He wasn't just facing death; many noble men have willingly faced a difficult death. Jesus was going to bear the sins of the world, take on all the pain of all the generations of mankind and do it without anger, bitterness, or hatred for those who killed Him. Jesus asked the Father if there was any way His cup could be taken from Him. This was not Jesus wimping out; it was Jesus in a real relationship with His Father, expressing His true feelings. Yet, as He prayed, He sensed the Father calling Him to this great

OVERVIEW

Jesus went to the garden of Gethsemane on the Mount of Olives to prepare for His arrest. He prayed in earnest to the Father while His disciples slept. Judas came and betrayed Him, and Jesus willingly went before the religious leaders to be accused so that He might obey God to the point of death.

SOURCE MATERIAL

- **Matthew 26:36-75**
- Psalm 55

task and responded, "...not as I will, but as You will" (Matt 26:39).

If there was any time that Jesus needed His disciples to stand beside Him, now was the time. But instead, they fell asleep, even after Jesus said, "My soul is exceedingly sorrowful, even to death. Stay here and watch with Me" (Matt 26:38). When He returned to find them sleeping, He rebuked them and told them that they needed to pray so they wouldn't fall into temptation. They didn't listen and fell asleep yet again (Matt 26:43). Their sleeping instead of praying foreshadows Peter's denial of Jesus and the fleeing of the disciples when Jesus was arrested. If they couldn't even pray in anticipation of a difficult experience, how could they stand when the temptation to run came?

At this point, Judas arrived to betray Jesus with a kiss (Matt 26:47). Judas had been the treasurer

Unit 5: Jesus' Final Days

OBJECTIVES

Feel...

- amazed at Jesus' calm in the face of His arrest and death.

Understand...

- that it was a great burden to Jesus to face bearing the sins of the world, but He was willing to do the Father's will.
- that the disciples' lack of vigilance led to their later denial of Jesus.
- that Judas was not *just* the bad guy—he was also Jesus' friend.
- that Peter didn't understand God's plan, so he cut off the servant's ear.
- why the religious leaders arrested Jesus at night.
- that Jesus willingly went along toward His death.
- that the priests couldn't come up with any case against Jesus.
- that all the disciples abandoned Jesus, with Peter denying Him three times.

Apply this understanding by...

- being prepared to pray when difficulties come to protect himself from temptation.

---

for Jesus and His followers, but wasn't truly a follower of Jesus. He *was* a friend, which made his betrayal of Jesus all the more painful. Earlier, he had gone to the chief priest and asked what He could get for handing Jesus over, and they agreed to 30 pieces of silver (Matt 26:14-16). Jesus knew what Judas was up to and had sent him off to do the job while they were still in the upper room (John 13:27). Upon Judas' arrival at the garden, he kissed Jesus to alert the armed men with him whom they were to arrest. Jesus' response was, "Do what you came for, friend" (Matt 26:50, NIV). And with that, they seized Him.

Peter was ready for a fight, drew his sword and cut off the ear of the high priest's servant (Matt 26:51). He meant to kill him, but his aim was a bit off. Peter didn't understand what Jesus was doing. Notice that Jesus didn't respond by saying that God's people never fight. In fact, earlier that night Jesus had told His disciples to sell their cloaks to buy swords (Luke 22:36). Peter was carrying a sword in obedience to Jesus, but now was not the time to use it. If Jesus had wanted to fight, He could have simply asked the Father to send legions of angels (Matt 26:53). Jesus had come to this time and place to submit Himself to death.

Jesus never intended to resist His arrest. Everyday He taught in the temple, and the priests left Him alone; but now they came after Him *at night*. Jesus called this out (Matt 26:55-56). The priests were afraid of the people. They knew that Jesus was a peaceful man and didn't dare arrest Him in public to protect themselves from the public outcry. At this point, the disciples deserted Jesus and fled (Matt 26:56).

It was now sometime in the middle of the night, and the Sanhedrin, the council of religious leaders, met at the house of the high priest, Caiaphas (Matt 26:57). They didn't have the authority to put anyone to death and needed a somewhat credible complaint to bring to the Roman authorities, so they attempted to hold some sort of a trial against Jesus. By holding this trial, the Sanhedrin were breaking every rule in their own book, but they went ahead with it anyway. The problem was that there was no *legitimate* com-

plaint against Jesus. They had to resort to false witnesses, but even the false witnesses couldn't come up with a charge that would stick. Finally, after messing around with witnesses for a while, the high priest asked Jesus directly and under oath if He was the Messiah. Jesus replied, "It is as you said" (Matt 26:64) and added a reference to the book of Daniel admitting that He was the Son of Man who would appear coming on the clouds of heaven. Jesus' words angered them and they decided, again without any real evidence, that He was worthy of death. Then they began to mock Him, hit Him and spit in His face (Matt 26:67-68).

Meanwhile, Peter had followed Jesus to Caiaphas' house and was sitting in the courtyard (Matt 26:69). Jesus had predicted that Peter would deny Him three times before the rooster crowed. In fulfillment of Jesus words, Peter denied Him three times and the final time with curses. Jesus had been betrayed by His friend, abandoned by His disciples, denied by Peter, arrested by the priests and had endured a mockery of a trial. He was on a mission of obedience to the Father and no matter what the cost to Himself, He would bear the sins of the world.

APPLICATION

The disciples knew that something big was about to happen from the way Jesus had been talking that night (John 13-16), but they failed in vigilance. They should have been praying, and Jesus even warned them; but instead, they slept. As a result, they weren't prepared when temptation came, and they fled from Jesus. Peter even denied that he knew Him.

Temptations to sin come with difficulties. Prayer—talking to the Father to see what He would have us do—is the antidote to these temptations. If you are not facing a trial right now, make a mental note for when the time of difficulty comes. It is important to cultivate a life of prayer even now so that you will also be in communion with the Father when difficulties come.

ACTIVITIES

1. Journal Time: Pray for Protection. Jesus spent time praying the night before His arrest. We too will face trials and temptation. It is important to learn to pray for protection against giving in to temptation during times of trial. In your the space below, spend some time writing out your prayer for protection against temptation. If you have a specific temptation you are currently struggling with, write about that, if you can't think of a specific temptation at this time, write for protection for the future.

_____
_____
_____

Lesson 5.5

EVALUATION

1. Why did Jesus ask for His cup to be taken away? Was He actually thinking of not going through with His death? _____

2. What was the impact of the disciples' lack of vigilance during the time they should have been praying in the garden? _____

3. Why did Peter cut off the servant's ear? What didn't he "get" that led to his violence? _____

4. Why did the religious leaders arrest Jesus at night? _____

5. What kind of accusations were brought against Jesus? _____

6. What happened to the disciples when Jesus was arrested? _____

LESSON 5.6

Jesus Tried and Convicted

UNIT 5

THE STORY

Lesson Theme - The people of Israel accepted the guilt of Jesus' blood.

Jesus' trial before Pilate and then Herod is a story of incredible buck-passing. The question hanging over this narrative is, "Who is going to take the responsibility for killing Jesus?" In the end, the blame landed squarely on the people of Israel.

Matthew 27 begins with the religious leaders bringing Jesus to Pilate, the Roman governor of the region. But then, in a somewhat surprising twist, Matthew interrupts the Pilate story and tells about Judas committing suicide (Matt 27:3-10). Judas realized what he had done, returned the money the priests had paid him and went out and killed himself. The religious leaders were to Pilate as Judas was to the religious leaders. Judas turned Jesus over to the religious leaders who then turned Jesus over to Pilate. Pilate now had the responsibility to bring Jesus to trial like the religious leaders had the night before.

The religious leaders wanted Jesus dead more than anyone, but they didn't want the responsibility for His death. They handed Jesus over to Pilate on political charges even though they didn't really care about Jesus' political claims (His claim to be King). They cared about His spiritual claims (His claim to be the Son of God), but used His political claims to bring charges against Him that would resonate with Pilate.

Pilate's question to Jesus reflected the political charges against Jesus that had been presented

OVERVIEW

The religious leaders took Jesus before Pilate, while Judas committed suicide for betraying an innocent man. The religious leaders wanted Jesus dead more than anyone, but they didn't want to take responsibility for killing Him. Pilate didn't want to take responsibility either; Jesus, however, put Pilate in the position of deciding whether or not He was King of the Jews. After trying to pass the buck, Pilate finally complied with the wishes of the people and sent Jesus off to be crucified. Pilate washed his hands of the thing, while the people took responsibility for Jesus' blood.

SOURCE MATERIAL

- **Matthew 27:1-31**
- Luke 23:4-12

to him, "Are you the king of the Jews?" (Matt 27:11a, NIV). Jesus' answer is puzzling. He didn't answer straightforwardly as He had when Caiaphas asked if He was the Messiah. Rather, He said, "You have said so" (Matt 27:11b, NIV). In other words, "I am not taking a stand on that point right now; the decision is in your hands as to whether or not I am the King." Jesus' response probably took the religious leaders by surprise as well, who probably expected Him to answer as straightforwardly with Pilate as He had done with them. In response, they reissued all their accusations against Him. But Jesus, to Pilate's

45

Unit 5: Jesus' Final Days

OBJECTIVES

Feel...

- intrigued by how Jesus chose to interact with the different authorities.
- surprised that the people of Israel took the responsibility for Jesus' blood.

Understand...

- that the religious leaders were to Pilate as Judas was to the religious leaders.
- that neither the religious leaders nor Pilate wanted to take the responsibility for Jesus' death.
- that Jesus' response to Pilate's question about Him being a king put Pilate in the position of king-maker.
- the ways that Pilate tried to avoid making a decision about Jesus:
  - by passing Him off to Herod.
  - by offering to release Him instead of Barabbas.
- that Pilate appealed to the people to get Jesus released.
- that the religious leaders successfully got the people to release Barabbas and call for Jesus' crucifixion.
- that the people took the responsibility for Jesus' blood on themselves.
- that Jesus was made King in mockery

Apply this understanding by...

- realizing that Jesus died for those who ultimately betrayed Him—the crowds who had followed Him—and therefore, He died for us who have betrayed Him through our sin; forgiveness is freely available to all.

---

great amazement, didn't respond to the charges, either denying them or affirming them.

This put Pilate in an interesting position and exactly the place Jesus was aiming for. Had Jesus just come out and said, "I am the King of the Jews," Pilate would have had no problem executing Him; Jesus would be claiming the position only Caesar was allowed over Israel. Instead, Pilate was in the position of king-maker. In order to crucify Jesus, he had to actually make Him King of the Jews.

Pilate didn't want to crucify Jesus and sought to get out of the responsibility of having to make that decision. He had a couple of things to try. First, he tried to pass the buck. Herod was the governor of Galilee; so when Pilate found out that Jesus was from Galilee, he sent Him over to Herod who happened to be in Jerusalem at the time. Herod was excited to meet Jesus and was hoping to see some sort of miracle, but Jesus didn't even speak to Herod. Finally, Herod grew tired of trying to talk to Jesus; so the Roman guards mocked Him, dressed Him in a royal robe and sent Him back to Pilate (Luke 23:8-12—this story is not told in Matthew).

Pilate's next attempt to avoid responsibility for Jesus' death was to try to free Jesus on grounds other than His innocence. It was customary for the governor to release a prisoner during the Passover feast (Matt 27:15). Barabbas was an actual criminal, so Pilate thought the Jewish people might want Jesus released rather than this dangerous man. Pilate knew that Jesus was popular among the crowds, so he bypassed the religious leaders (whom he knew would not want Jesus released) and went directly to the people. Somewhat surprisingly, the religious leaders had been able to convince the crowd to release Barabbas (Matt 27:20).

Unit 5: Jesus' Final Days

You might even say it worked too well. Remember, no one in any position of authority wanted to take responsibility for crucifying Jesus. Judas realized what he had done and said, "I have sinned...for I have betrayed innocent blood" (Matt 27:4a, NIV). To which the religious leaders *did not* say, "Hey, we were in on it too"; they let the responsibility fall on Judas, saying, "What is that to us? That's your responsibility" (Matt 27:4b, NIV). Likewise, Pilate now passed the responsibility on to the people, who were demanding that Jesus be crucified. "I am innocent of this man's blood," he said. "It is your responsibility!" (Matt 27:24b, NIV). Neither Pilate nor the religious leaders would take the responsibility for killing Jesus, *even though they were the ones making the decision*. But the people happily took the blame, "His blood is on us and on our children!" (Matt 27:25, NIV).

This sounds bad, and it is, but it also gives us hope. Ironically, since the people and their children took full responsibility for Jesus' blood, it also opened up the possibility for them and future generations to receive the forgiveness that His blood secured and is freely available to all. There is no forgiveness for those who have done no wrong.

It was official; Jesus was going to be crucified. The Roman soldiers led Him off and began to "make" Him King. The soldiers' mockery was more true than they knew. They put a king's robe on Him, a crown on His head and a staff in His hand and began bowing down before Him in mockery (Matt 27:28-29).

APPLICATION

The application for this lesson is simply to observe that Jesus died for those who killed Him. In the end, the people of Israel, the crowds who flocked after Him, those who experienced His healing touch, were the ultimate betrayers. They took the blame for His blood; Pilate and the religious leaders never pretended to like Jesus and took no responsibility. It was those people, the great crowd of Judases who took His blood on their hands, whom Jesus died to forgive.

Likewise, we are sinners, and would've crucified Jesus had we been in that crowd. Many of these people would hear Peter preach in little more than a month and repent and believe. They knew what they did, and they found that Jesus died for it. We too are freely called to repent and believe whenever we wander from the Lord, because He died for our sins too.

Lesson 5.6

ACTIVITIES

1. Reflection: Responsible Parties. In this story there are many responsible parties to Jesus' death. Only the people and Judas took the blame, but many more had a hand in it. Fill in the table below, writing how each different person or group of people were guilty of Jesus' death and what they might have done differently.

Guilty Party	How were they guilty?	What could they have done differently?
Judas		
The Religious Leaders		
The People		
Pilate		
Herod		
The Roman Guards		
The Disciples		

Unit 5: Jesus' Final Days

2. Jesus Made King. In this lesson, we learned how the Roman soldiers mockingly made Jesus King; they didn't realize that their actions done in mockery were actually things that are true of Jesus. Read Matthew 27:27-29 and list all the things the soldiers did in mockery to make Jesus King. Then, match each of the things the soldiers did with one of the verses below that predicts Jesus' kingship in a glorious, non-mocking way.

Genesis 49:10

Philippians 2:10

Revelation 14:14

Revelation 19:13

List of ways the soldiers mocked Jesus	Corresponding verse of Jesus' Kingship

Lesson 5.6

EVALUATION

1. In what way were the religious leaders like Judas? _____
_____

2. Pilate asked Jesus if He was King of the Jews and Jesus said, "You have said so" (Matt 27:11b, NIV). What was the effect of this? Was it an admission of being King?_____
_____
_____

3. What did Pilate do to avoid making a decision about Jesus? _____
_____
_____

4. What finally convinced Pilate to give the go-ahead to kill Jesus?_____
_____

5. Who ended up taking responsibility for Jesus' death?_____
_____

6. What happened to Jesus after Pilate sent Him off to be crucified?_____
_____

LESSON 5.7

Jesus' Crucifixion and Burial

UNIT 5

THE STORY

Lesson Theme - Jesus crushed the serpent's head on the cross.

This lesson is about the suffering of the Messiah. The overarching theme of this curriculum is head-crushing, and the Messiah is the ultimate head-crusher. But Genesis 3:15 says two things about the the Messiah: (1) He would crush the head of the serpent, and (2) His heel would be bruised *by* the serpent. In this lesson, we see Satan at what appears to be his finest hour, the hour when he thought he had won. By all appearances, Jesus being mocked, beaten and hung on the cross was the most bitter defeat He could possibly have faced.

This lesson and the next lesson (on the resurrection) are the high points of the entire biblical Story and the culmination of two of the most significant themes in this curriculum (and, for that matter, in the Bible). These are the themes of head-crushing and baptism. We will tie the theme of head-crushing to this lesson and the theme of baptism to the next lesson.

Before we get into the content of this lesson, we need to do a little review. Jesus is here fulfilling the head-crushing theme that we began exploring in the first lessons of the Old Testament curriculum. So for review, we are going to start with Genesis 3:15 and work our way through scripture with this theme in mind in order to tie it all together at the cross.

OVERVIEW

The entirety of the Old Testament points toward the coming Messiah as the final head-crusher. Jesus' disciples were expecting Jesus to defeat their enemies and take His rightful place as King. Instead, He was mocked, beaten, crucified and buried. He received the fate of the serpent in order to defeat the serpent once and for all.

SOURCE MATERIAL

- **Matthew 27:32-66**
- Mark 15:21-47
- Luke 23:26-56
- John 19:16-42

The head-crushing theme through the Bible
In the beginning God created a home for mankind to live in and rule over. He put the man in a garden and gave the woman as a helper. They could eat from any tree in the garden, but the tree of the knowledge of good and evil was forbidden.

The serpent tricked Eve into eating from this tree by convincing her that God was withholding something good. Adam and Eve gave their authority to the serpent and fell out of relationship with God. But the Story doesn't end there; God promised that a seed of the woman would crush the serpent's head, bruising His own heel in the process and restoring mankind to his proper rule over creation.

Unit 5: Jesus' Final Days

OBJECTIVES

Feel...

- the uncomfortable incongruity between the prophecies of Jesus as the head-crusher and the fact that He was crucified.
- sadness at the crucifixion of Christ.
- awe at the awesome power displayed when Jesus died.

Understand...

- the story of the head-crushers leading up to Christ.
- how surprising Christ's death was in light of the whole biblical narrative.
- that Jesus' death was absolutely necessary to defeat death and the serpent.
- that Jesus' resurrection transformed Jesus' death from defeat to victory.
- that Jesus died when and where we expected the serpent to die in order to defeat the power of death.
- that Jesus also died in the place of all mankind who, through Adam and Eve's rebellion, had chosen to follow the serpent.
- that when Simon of Cyrene carried the cross of Christ, he was showing us what discipleship means.

Apply this understanding by...

- identifying ways you can take up your cross daily to die with Christ.

Adam and Eve's first son, Cain, murdered their second son, Abel, so God provided Seth; Seth's righteous line replaced Cain's wicked line. Seth's descendant, Noah, was righteous at a time when the whole earth was wicked. So God destroyed the earth with a flood and made a covenant with Noah. God confused the languages of Noah's descendants to scatter them throughout the earth, but He did not forget His promise, and the seed-line was established from Shem to Abraham.

Through Abraham, God created Israel, the seed-nation. Abraham moved into the promised land and proved to be a head-crusher. When the land was attacked by the surrounding nations, Abraham pursued the aggressors and delivered the Canaanites. His victory made him a sort of head-crushing king over Canaan.

God provided Abraham with a son-of-promise, Isaac, who had a son named Jacob, or Israel, the father of the twelve tribes. Jacob's sons were a wicked bunch, but Judah grew in righteousness. Ultimately, he offered his life in place of his brother Benjamin's. When famine struck, the whole family moved to Egypt. Here, Jacob blessed Judah and called him a lion whose hand would be on the neck of his enemies and from whom the ruling scepter would not depart. Judah was the father of the coming head-crusher.

The family of Jacob multiplied in Egypt and were enslaved to Pharaoh. When God saw their oppression, He caused a son to be born and miraculously preserved, a deliverer for the people of Israel: Moses. Moses was a born head-crusher; he killed an Egyptian for beating an Israelite. He fled to Midian where he met God. Despite Moses' objections, God used him to crush Pharaoh and deliver Israel out of slavery.

God delivered the people of Israel, but they faltered in the wilderness, doubting God's power to crush the heads of the Canaanites and complaining against the Lord. So God raised up Joshua. He led the second generation into Israel, and they went about the land, defeating the Canaanites. On one occasion, Joshua trapped five kings, stepped on their necks, hung them on trees, and cast their bodies into a cave which he covered with stones. Joshua was the head-crushing conquerer of the Canaanite kings.

Israel's victory over the land was substantial, but not complete. Following Joshua's conquest, a series of judges and head-crushing women delivered Israel from the remaining Canaanites in the land. Ehud killed Eglon. Samson crushed 1,000 Philistine heads with the jawbone of a donkey and then crushed the five kings of the Philistines when he knocked down their temple. Jael drove a tent peg through Sisera's head, and a woman threw an upper millstone off a tower to crush the head of Abimelech. But the people faltered again and took the ark into battle as if it were a magic charm. God repaid their lack of faith with defeat. The Philistines captured the ark and placed it before their god, Dagon. In the morning, they found Dagon's head lying broken before the ark. God is the true head-crusher.

Following the judges, Saul was made king of Israel, but he turned out to be a disobedient coward. David succeeded him after crushing the head of Goliath with a small stone. God promised that David's line would rule over Israel forever. Solomon succeeded David as king and reigned during a time of peace and rest. Ultimately, however, Solomon turned to foreign gods. After Solomon's death, the nation was divided and the kings were wicked, so God gave the people to their enemies as slaves. They repented and returned to the land, but things weren't the same. They longed for the time when the promised Deliverer would come, one who would conquer their oppressors and bring peace to Israel.

Into this conflicted nation, Jesus was born. Israel was a nation longing for a king, but under the tyranny of the Romans. Like many head-crushers before Him, Jesus' birth was both miraculous and humble. And He proved to be a head-crusher indeed, by casting out demons, healing disease, castigating the established authorities, and welcoming a virtual army of diverse followers. But His own people, especially the religious leaders, turned against Him because He challenged their authority and because His kingdom wasn't what they expected.

What happened next was so backwards, shocking, and contrary to people's expectations, that Jesus was abandoned by almost all of His followers. Instead of the serpent ending up on the cross, the head-crusher was there. Instead of a stone being rolled in front of the enemy's tomb, it covered the tomb of the seed-king.

This is poaching on the next lesson a bit, but there is no way of understanding the significance of the crucifixion without making an appeal to the resurrection. If the resurrection had never occurred, the crucifixion would've been the biggest let-down of all time. However, in light of the resurrection, in the crucifixion, Jesus crushed the head of the murderer. But not only that; Jesus crushed murder itself. Death has no power over the Son of God who received the fate of the serpent to destroy the serpent once and for all. He ascended into heaven and sits at the right hand of God the Father almighty, whence He shall come back to judge the living and the dead. And He shall reign over the house of Jacob forever; and of His kingdom there shall be no end.

Jesus is our substitute
We stated above that Jesus "received the fate of the serpent to destroy the serpent once and for all." This may sound like a strange idea, but

it is exactly what the Bible teaches. Numbers 21 records how God sent serpents among the Israelites because of their wickedness. The serpent bites were deadly, but God provided a way out. He had Moses make a bronze serpent and hang it on a pole. If the people looked at it and believed, they would live. The symbolism is pretty straightforward: the serpents were the source of evil and death, and the bronze serpent was a picture of God's power over these evil creatures—after all, it was a *dead* serpent on a pole. The Israelites were believing in God's power over the serpent.

Jesus said, "And as Moses lifted up the serpent in the wilderness, even so must the Son of Man be lifted up, that whoever believes in Him should not perish but have everlasting life." (John 3:14-15). Jesus died in the place of the serpent, knowing that the only way to defeat the serpent was to take the power of death away from him. The way to take the power of death away from the serpent was to die at his hand and then raise from the dead.

When Adam and Eve ate from the tree of the knowledge of good and evil at the serpent's urging, they rebelled against God and aligned themselves with the serpent. This means that just as Jesus died right when the Story had led us to expect the serpent would die, He also died right when Adam and Eve should have—and when all those who inherited the disease of sin from Adam and Eve should have died. For the serpent, Jesus' death and resurrection meant that the power of death had been taken from him. For us, it means that death's power *over us* is taken away... "that whoever believes in Him should not perish but have eternal life" (John 3:15).

Jesus' crucifixion, death and burial
When Jesus' death is discussed today, often the subject of the physical pain and suffering that He endured comes to the forefront. However, Matthew (and the other gospel writers for that matter) focuses not on the brutality of Jesus' death, but on the mockery and humiliation He endured in the process of His crucifixion. His claim to be King was mocked, He was crucified like a common criminal alongside common criminals, and even the criminals mocked Him!

The irony in the mockery is that so many of the mocking comments spoken to Jesus were actually true and fitting praise for the great sacrifice He was making. The soldiers stripped Him, put on a scarlet robe and placed a crown of thorns on His head. He was crowned King *while* He was dying for His people, the ultimate kingly act.

Jesus underwent such torture that He was unable to carry His cross to where He would be crucified. Simon of Cyrene was compelled by the Roman officials to carry the cross of Christ. In all likelihood, this Simon was a Christian, or later became one, since he is mentioned by name. Mark notes that he was the father of Alexander and Rufus who must've been known to the Christian community Mark was writing to. Regardless, the act of carrying the cross of Christ is a profound picture of discipleship. We are called to participate in Jesus' suffering for the glory of God.

Jesus' enemies *tried* to make His crucifixion a common event, like the crucifixion of a common criminal. And it was working pretty well... up until He was on the cross with His death approaching, and darkness overcame the land *in the middle of the afternoon.* Then, when Jesus died, the earth quaked, graves were opened and the dead emerged. At this point, even the centurion who oversaw Jesus' crucifixion believed in Him.

Jesus was buried in the tomb of Joseph of Arimathea, one of Jesus' disciples who wanted to ensure that Jesus received a proper burial. Jesus was placed in the tomb, like so many others before Him, and a large stone was rolled in front of the grave. In response to the request of the Pharisees, who were concerned that Jesus' body might be taken by His followers, Pilate placed guards in front of the tomb. The Son of God was dead.

APPLICATION

Jesus died for us, and now we are called to die with Him. This is not a quid pro quo exchange, as though we have to now pay Jesus back for what He did for us on the cross. Rather, when Jesus died on the cross, those who have believed *did* die with Him; we were united with Him in His death. Now we are called to daily die with Christ—not to pay Him back, but to live out our identity in Christ. We must, like Simon of Cyrene, take up our cross daily and follow Him.

You may not really know yet what it means to die with Christ. Or perhaps you do, maybe you've had hard experiences that have given you a taste. The practical output for this is really in the Lord's hands; we don't decide the circumstances under which we will have to give up our personal desires and ambitions to be obedient to Christ and suffer along with Him. But we can prepare ourselves through faithfulness and prayer to face those times. Preparation for those more serious times of "dying" comes through daily dying to our sinful desires.

ACTIVITIES

1. Painting Interpretation. Carefully examine the painting on the following page of the moment that Christ died. Try and see the hidden meanings and symbolism in the painting and write down your thoughts. _____

_____

_____

_____

_____

_____

_____

_____

_____

Lesson 5.7

EVALUATION

1. We all know the Bible well enough to know that the hero died right at the climax, but the disciples had no idea that this would happen—why? _____

_____

_____

2. Why did Jesus have to die to defeat the serpent? _____

_____

_____

3. How did the disciples see Jesus' death at the time? How did they see it after the resurrection? _____

_____

_____

4. What does Simon of Cyrene's act of carrying the cross teach us about discipleship? _____

_____

LESSON 5.8

Jesus' Resurrection and Ascension

THE STORY

Lesson Theme - The risen Savior
The resurrection is the high point, the turning point in the Story. Death had been crying out for a solution since Adam and Eve rebelled, and in this lesson we get it. It's a big deal. As in the last lesson, we will chase a biblical theme through the entire Bible: the theme of baptism. The biblical theme of baptism has been pointing to the need for an ultimate resurrection all along. Baptism is a picture of death and resurrection and it is *the* unifying structure of all the little biblical stories leading up to this ultimate resurrection.

Take some time to meditate on the following baptism theme before you dig into the Bible passages that talk about the resurrection. In order to get a taste of the disciples' experienced of the resurrection, you need to grasp the full weight of baptism as deeply as they did.

The story of the baptized deliverer from Genesis to Jesus
In the beginning God created the earth—unformed and covered with water. The Spirit hovered over the surface of the water. Then, at God's command, land and life emerged from under the water as though rising from the dead. The Lord made a garden and placed Adam and Eve in it to be rulers over the world. A river ran through the garden from the throne of God, bringing life wherever it flowed. But ultimately, Adam and Eve chose death over life when the serpent deceived them and they disobeyed God. However, the Story doesn't end there;

OVERVIEW

The whole Bible points to the need for resurrection—for water to wash over all things and transform death into life. When Jesus' body was put in the grave, His disciples thought that the end of their hope had come, but it was only the beginning. Jesus rose from the dead and appeared to many; therefore, we have hope.

SOURCE MATERIAL

- **John 20:1-21:14**
- Matthew 28
- Mark 16
- Luke 24

God promised that a seed of the woman would crush the serpent's head—sin and death would be destroyed, and all of creation would be given new life.

Adam's descendants were evil, so evil, in fact, that God chose to start over with Noah. Water brought God's judgement of death to the earth, and the renewed world emerged out of the water. God saved Noah and his family through the water, and they became rulers over the new creation. But creation awaited a more perfect resurrection, one to which Noah's flood points.

Through one of Noah's descendants, Abram, God created a people who would become a baptized and resurrected nation, called to bring light to

Unit 5: Jesus' Final Days

OBJECTIVES

Feel...

- joy that Jesus was raised from the dead.
- hope—in our own resurrection and the resurrection of all things.

Understand...

- the thread of baptism that runs through the entire biblical narrative.
- that baptism is a death and resurrection theme.
- that the theme of baptism pointed all along to Jesus' death and resurrection.
- that Jesus' resurrection transformed Jesus' death from defeat to victory.
- when the disciples "got it"—Peter and John when they saw the empty tomb, Mary when she met Jesus in the garden, and the rest when He appeared to them.
- that Jesus' resurrection was in bodily form.
- that we have hope of our own resurrection in Christ—and the resurrection of all things.

Apply this understanding by...

- living out your hope and finding a way to pray for resurrection to come to the world around you.

the world. God provided Abraham with a son-of-promise, Isaac, who had a son named Jacob, or Israel, the father of the twelve tribes of Israel. On account of a famine in the land, the twelve tribes moved to Egypt, where they were granted favor.

As time passed, the family of Jacob multiplied in Egypt and were perceived as a threat by Pharaoh. Pharaoh enslaved the Israelites and commanded that all the newborn boys be killed. When God saw their oppression, He caused Moses to be born and miraculously preserved through water—Moses experienced a sort of baptism on an "ark" in the Nile.

God preserved Moses for a purpose—to become a deliverer for Israel. He called him into the wilderness for a time of training. Then Moses returned to Egypt and delivered Israel from slavery, led them on dry ground under the surface of the sea and raised them to new life as a nation on the other side.

This new nation, baptized in the Red Sea, also received a new Law to govern their community and their worship of the Lord. To administer the worship of God, the priests were to be baptized. Their baptism symbolized their own personal re-creation; the priest was a normal member of Israel before the baptism; but after, he was a member of a new people with a new identity and new rights and responsibilities in his relationship with God.

The first generation of Israel after the exodus doubted and complained against the Lord. So God raised up Joshua. He led the second generation into Israel through a new baptism in the Jordan and into conquest in the land where they defeated the Canaanites and took control of the land.

For a time, Israel lived in the land in a cycle of death and resurrection. They would turn from the Lord, be subjected to slavery in the land until they repented, cry out to the Lord for deliverance, and God would then send a judge to defeat their enemies and free Israel to worship Him again. Finally, they would walk with the Lord for a time until they turned to idols again; their resurrection was always temporary.

When God gave Israel a king, a similar pattern of death and resurrection prevailed. A good king would restore Israel to proper worship of God for a time; then a wicked king would turn the nation to idols. Over time, the nation was divided and fell into deeper and deeper idolatry. Finally, God exiled Israel from the land, but after 70 years, He had mercy on His people and brought them back into the land and into new life once again. Jerusalem and the temple were rebuilt, and worship of God resumed.

Israel never turned to literal idols again, but they made an idol out of the Law and the hope of the kingdom. They fought hard to gain independence from their foreign conquerors, but turned from the living God of the Bible. The religious leaders—those who operated the temple—were the most hard-hearted of all. This was a nation that needed new life; they needed to be baptized.

God sent John, known as the Baptizer, to bring this new life to Israel and prepare for the Messiah. John called Israel to the wilderness to be baptized in the Jordan like they had in the days of Joshua; but instead of entering the land as a new nation, they were being separated from the old Israel and made into a new people in Christ. John even baptized the Messiah—in whom all who were baptized would find their identity.

Jesus' baptism pointed to a way of living—a life of death and resurrection. Throughout His ministry, He called the lost to find new life in Him; He called them to lay down their own desires, hopes and dreams so that they could inherit even greater glory. In the new people that Jesus created, suffering always preceded glory; death always preceded new life—this was what baptism had been pointing to all along.

Inevitably (though no one could see it then) Jesus' whole life was pointing to the necessity that He too must die. The Son of God would go through His own baptism—death and resurrection—to crush the head of the serpent in death and to secure the ultimate hope for all mankind in resurrection.

After our Lord went to the cross, He told His disciples to "Go therefore and make disciples of all the nations, baptizing them in the name of the Father and of the Son and of the Holy Spirit, teaching them to observe all things that I have commanded you; and lo, I am with you always, even to the end of the age" (Matt 28:19-20). Then He ascended into heaven and sits at the right hand of God the Father almighty, whence He shall come back to judge the living and the dead. And He shall reign over the house of Jacob forever; and of His kingdom there shall be no end.

The resurrection
The disciples as well as the women who walked with Jesus were absolutely broken by His death. They had no way of making sense of it. Of course, as we saw in the baptism theme, Jesus' death was truly inevitable, but not in a way that someone inside the Story could see. They had lost their Lord and Master; they had lost their hope; but, perhaps even more relevant that Sunday morning, they had lost a loved one, a friend. Mary went to the tomb, not hoping that she would find Him there alive, but to mourn His loss. When she saw that His body wasn't there, she assumed that it had been stolen, so that's what she told Peter and John (John 20:1-2).

Unit 5: Jesus' Final Days

When Peter and John heard that Jesus' body was missing, they ran to the tomb; and when John stepped in the tomb and saw the cloth that had wrapped Jesus still lying in position, he believed (John 20:8). The whole Story had been pointing to Jesus' resurrection (John 20:9), but they had missed it. Now seeing the empty tomb, it all made sense; in a moment they went from unbelief to belief in the risen Lord.

Mary had apparently returned to the tomb with Peter and John and now stood outside the tomb in the garden. When she saw Jesus, she mistook Him for the gardener, which was exactly the right mistake to make (John 20:15). The gospel of John is pointing us back to the garden of Eden where Adam, the first gardener, was put to sleep, had a rib taken out of him and a woman presented to him when he awoke. In this little iconic picture, Jesus is the new Adam, and Mary represents the new Eve, the Church. Jesus had gone to sleep and awoke to meet this woman in the garden. But it was not yet time for the wedding; Jesus said, "Do not cling to Me, for I have not yet ascended to My Father" (John 20:17).

That evening Jesus appeared to the disciples in the room where they were hiding with the doors locked. The first thing He said to them was, "Peace be with you" (John 20:19). Then He breathed on them, giving them the gift of the Holy Spirit and authority to forgive sins. Jesus was sent by the Father and now He was sending the disciples out with the presence of the Holy Spirit.

Awhile later, Jesus appeared to several of the disciples by the Sea of Galilee (John 21:1). While they were out fishing, Jesus appeared on the shore and told them to cast their nets on the other side of the boat so that they would catch some fish. The disciples obeyed and brought in a large catch of fish. When they came to shore, Jesus made them breakfast.

This story shows us two things. First, it gives us a picture, or a taste, of how the disciples' relationship with the Lord Jesus would be once He ascended. In Luke 5, Jesus called the disciples to be fishers of men and told them to cast their nets on the other side of the boat. When they did, their nets came up full. The main difference between the miracle in Luke 5 and the miracle in John 21 is that Jesus was on the boat with them the first time; but the second time, He was directing them from the shore. When Jesus ascended, we did not lose His guidance, but we did lose His bodily presence. Not long after this event, Jesus ascended and left the disciples to fish for men without Him in the "boat" (on earth), but His guidance was still theirs from "the shore" (heaven).

The second point to draw out of this circumstance is the fact that Jesus ate with His disciples after His resurrection. Ghost's don't eat fish—Jesus' resurrection was a physical, bodily resurrection.

The hope of the resurrection
Jesus' bodily resurrection points to our own hope. This really is the biggest lesson from the resurrection—this hope is the good news of Christianity, and yet so few Christians understand it.

Most Christians believe that the Christian hope boils down to the fact that we will be in Jesus' presence in heaven when we die. True, we will go to heaven to be in the presence of Jesus when we die. But, without fail, the New Testament points toward a more ultimate hope—one in which our physical, glorified bodies will be resurrected; our spirits will be reunited with our bodies; the earth will be healed and we will be restored to our original purpose on the earth—to be kings and queens over God's creation. Jesus' physical resurrection and the fact that He could walk around on the earth and eat fish assure us that this day is coming. We *will* be raised from the dead to return to the earth and rule over it.

In other words, the Christian hope is *life after life after death*. Heaven is only a temporary holding place for believers. Ultimately, heaven will come to earth at the end of the age and God's purposes for mankind will be restored.

This may not sound like a terribly important distinction, but it has significant implications. Believing that heaven is our ultimate hope tends to produce an escapist attitude toward this world. At worst, this belief manifests in a mentality that doesn't care to accomplish anything for the Lord; at best, it produces a mentality that says, "Let's just save as many as we can before we die or the Lord returns." This belief is not likely to produce a "Thy kingdom come" mentality. And this kingdom-centered mentality is what we are aiming for—if Jesus rose from the dead, then everything in this world will be redeemed; our work now is good for eternity.

APPLICATION

The main take-home from this lesson has to do with learning to walk in resurrection hope. Jesus *is* raised from the dead. His resurrection is the firstfruits of our own resurrection, it is a piece of the future pulled into the present. The world around us is broken; the people around us are broken. Jesus *was* broken, but now He is whole; and because this is true it means that we, and all things, will one day be made whole.

For those who believe in Jesus, the hope of the resurrection is not just a future event. It is present; the resurrected Jesus lives in us, so we walk in this world as those who hold the resurrection within. Jesus, even before His resurrection, taught His followers to pray, "Thy kingdom come, Thy will be done, on earth as it is in heaven." This is a prayer for bits and pieces of the resurrection to break forth around us, and God has allowed us to be agents of this resurrection.

But let's be clear about this: the kingdom coming around us does not come based on our effort any more than our new birth happened by our effort. It is miraculous, and it is all a work of the Spirit. But God, in His great plan, has ordained that His Spirit would dwell in us and the kingdom would come through our agency as we pray and trust in Him to do the miraculous around us.

Walking in the resurrection means finding a place of brokenness around us and praying specifically for resurrection in that area. A friend who is sick, a neighbor who doesn't know the Lord, a torn relationship with a family member. God answers our specific prayers to see His kingdom come.

Unit 5: Jesus' Final Days

ACTIVITIES

1. Journal Time: Walking in the Resurrection. Spend some time in prayer, asking God to reveal an area of death around you—anything that doesn't fit into God's kingdom—that needs resurrection. It might be a need for physical healing, a relational problem with your family or friends, or someone's need to hear the gospel. After hearing from the Lord, in the space below write out a short (one or two sentence) specific prayer relating to that area. Then, pray that prayer every day until God answers it.

The area of death that needs resurrection:_____

_____

My specific prayer:_____

_____

_____

2. Hope of Heaven vs. Hope of the Resurrection. Answer the following questions about heaven and the resurrection.

What happens to people after they die? _____

_____

_____

What is heaven for? What are we going to do there? _____

_____

_____

Are we ever going to leave heaven, or is that our permanent home? _____

_____

_____

Will we ever be reunited with our bodies like Jesus was when He rose from the dead? Or will we forever be bodiless spirits in heaven?_____

_____

_____

_____

Lesson 5.8

Read Revelation 21, and write down some of your thoughts about it below. _____
_____
_____
_____
_____

EVALUATION

1. The disciples were not expecting Jesus to die, and once He died, they didn't know that He would be resurrected. We wouldn't have gotten it had we been them, but what big hint in the Bible points toward Jesus' death and resurrection? _____
_____
_____

2. What does Jesus' resurrection mean for the serpent?_____
_____
_____

3. When did the disciples believe that Jesus had risen from the dead?_____
_____
_____
_____

4. Describe Jesus after the resurrection._____
_____

5. What does the resurrection mean for us?_____
_____
._____

6. Where will we go when we die?_____

7. Will we stay there forever? What happens next? _____
_____

www.ingramcontent.com/pod-product-compliance
Lightning Source LLC
Chambersburg PA
CBHW081339080526
44588CB00017B/2680